SEA MAMMALS

Jen Green

Grolier
an imprint of

www.scholastic.com/librarypublishing

Published 2009 by Grolier
An Imprint of Scholastic Library Publishing
Old Sherman Turnpike
Danbury, Connecticut 06816

For The Brown Reference Group plc
Project Editor: Jolyon Goddard
Picture Researcher: Clare Newman
Designer: Sarah Williams
Managing Editor: Tim Harris

Volume ISBN-13: 978-0-7172-8053-7
Volume ISBN-10: 0-7172-8053-5

**Library of Congress
Cataloging-in-Publication Data**

Nature's children. Set 5.
    p. cm.
  Includes index.
  ISBN-13: 978-0-7172-8084-1
  ISBN-10: 0-7172-8084-5 (set)
  1. Animals--Encyclopedias, Juvenile. I.
Grolier Educational (Firm)
  QL49.N386 2009
  590.3--dc22
                          2008014674

Printed and bound in China

PICTURE CREDITS

Front Cover: **Shutterstock**: Ivan Histand.

Back Cover: **NaturePL**: Doug Perrine;
Shutterstock: Charlie Bishop, Jan Daly,
Kristian Sekulic.

FLPA: Flip Nicklin 30, 37, Konrad Wothe 33;
NaturePL: Mark Cawardine 18, Sue Flood
29, Frei/ARCO 46, Jurgen Freund 14, Doug
Perrine 4, 6, 13, Gabriel Rojo 34, Jeff Rotman
22, David Tipling 9, Staffan Widstrand 10;
Photolibrary: John Hyde 38, Emil Thor
Sigurdsson 41, James Watt 17; **Shutterstock**:
Charlie Bishop 42, Edward Chin 26–27, Four
Oaks 2–3, Emin Kuliyev 21, Jan Martin Will 5;
Still Pictures: Franco Banfi 45.

Contents

FACT FILE: Sea Mammals

Class	Mammals (Mammalia)
Orders	Whales, dolphins, and porpoises (Cetacea); seals, sea lions, and the walrus (Carnivora); manatees and the dugong (Sirenia)
Families	19 families
Genera	63 genera
Species	About 126 species
World distribution	All seas and oceans; some dolphins live in rivers; one seal lives in a lake
Habitat	Shallow and deep seas and oceans; some spend time out of the sea on coasts and ice; some live in freshwater
Distinctive physical characteristics	Sea mammals have a body built for swimming with finlike limbs called flippers and often a horizontal tail; many have thick blubber to keep them warm in cold water
Habits	Many swim long distances for food or to breed; seals and sea lions breed on land or on ice; whales, dolphins, and sea cows spend their whole life in water
Diet	Varies with species—seaweed, sea grasses, mollusks, shellfish, krill, fish, penguins, and other sea mammals

Introduction

What do seals, whales, and dolphins have in common? They are all sea **mammals**. The group of water-living mammals also includes the walrus, porpoises, and sea cows. Many sea mammals have a streamlined body and a powerful tail. They look very similar to fish such as sharks, but they are certainly not fish! In fact, they belong to the animal group that includes dogs, cats, horses, monkeys—and humans.

Sea mammals are clever creatures. They have starred in movies and are able to perform complicated tricks. However there are many things humans still do not know about sea mammals. That is mainly because it's not easy to study these animals closely in their watery world.

On ice, a leopard seal shows off its sharp teeth.

A Hawaiian monk seal's streamlined body shape allows it to twist and turn acrobatically underwater.

6

Shape and Size

Sea mammals come in a variety of sizes. Some, such as seals, are quite small. The smallest seals are about 4 feet (1.2 m) long. However, that is still large compared to many land mammals, such as rabbits, guinea pigs, and mice. The great whales are the largest living things on Earth. The biggest, the blue whale, grows to an enormous 100 feet (30 m) long and can weigh 170 tons (170 tonnes).

Whatever their size, all sea mammals have a sleek, or streamlined, body shape that slips easily through water—like a speedboat. Instead of legs and arms like humans, marine mammals have **flippers** and most have a powerful tail that propels them through the water. Whales and dolphins also have a fin on their back, which helps them steer. The back limbs of sea mammals are often small, such as in seals, or cannot be seen at all, such as in whales and dolphins.

Land and Sea

Marine mammals may look very different from land mammals—such as cats and elephants—but all mammals have certain things in common. They are all "warm-blooded." That means their body stays at the same temperature no matter what the temperature of their surroundings is. Being warm-blooded allows mammals to be active all year—unlike some cold-blooded animals that have to **hibernate** in winter. To achieve that, mammals need a lot of food. Sea mammals also have a thick layer of fatty **blubber** beneath their skin to keep them warm in cold water. Seals have a dense coat of fur, too—just like land mammals that live in cold places.

Like all mammals, baby sea mammals are born alive, rather than hatching from eggs like most types of fish, frogs, and reptiles. Seals and walruses give birth on land or on sea ice. Whales, dolphins, and sea cows give birth in water. Like all baby mammals, these youngsters drink their mother's milk.

8

This northern fur seal has come ashore in Alaska. Its fur coat and layer of blubber keep it warm in the chilly Arctic seas.

9

In water, a walrus's skin is gray. But in the sun, blood vessels in the skin expand, turning it hot pink!

Where in the World?

As a group, sea mammals are found in every part of the oceans. Some, such as small whales called belugas and narwhals, swim in icy Arctic waters. Others, such as many types of dolphins, prefer the warm seas of the tropics.

Marine mammals such as whales travel huge distances through the oceans. Each year they move between their regular feeding grounds and the sheltered waters where they breed. These journeys are called **migrations**. The gray whale is one of the greatest travelers. A gray whale can swim up to 12,500 miles (20,000 km) in a year.

Seals, sea lions, and walruses generally swim in coastal waters and spend a lot of time on land, basking in the sun. However, whales, dolphins, and sea cows never leave the water. Some of them spend their life in the open ocean and rarely come in sight of land.

Breathing in Water

Fish have **gills**, which allow them to absorb oxygen directly from the water. However, seals, whales, and other sea mammals do not have gills. Instead, they have lungs, like other mammals. Therefore, most sea mammals have to surface every two to twenty minutes, depending on the type, to breathe life-giving air. But some whales, such as deep-diving sperm whales, can stay underwater for more than one hour before having to come up for a fresh breath.

Seals and walruses breathe through their mouth and nostrils, just like humans do. That suits them because they spend a lot of time on land. Whales and dolphins spend their whole life at sea. They breathe through **blowholes** on the top of their head. The blowhole acts as a nostril. Whales and dolphins, therefore, don't have to lift their whole head out of the water to take in air.

A false killer whale—a large type of dolphin—breathes out through its blowhole.

13

A whale's eyes are located on the sides of its head so it cannot see directly in front of itself.

Finding Food

Most sea mammals feed on meat of some kind, which may be fish, squid, tiny shrimp, or even other sea mammals. However, sea cows are vegetarians. They feed only on seaweed and water plants. Whether meat or plant eaters, sea mammals' senses are fine-tuned to finding food in water. Seals track down fish using their large eyes and well-developed hearing. Walruses use the sensitive whiskers above their mouth to feel for shellfish in the mud.

Many whales, including dolphins, have small eyes. Eyesight—no matter how good it is—is not much use for tracking **prey** in murky water. Instead, these animals rely on sound. They send out a stream of clicking sounds that spread out through the surrounding water. The sounds bounce back when they hit an object such as a fish. By listening to the echoes, the whale or dolphin pinpoints its prey. This technique is called **echolocation**. It also helps the mammal find its way through narrow spaces such as between rocks.

Two Families

Dolphins and porpoises are two families of toothed whales. Although the two groups are hard to tell apart, there are some telltale differences. Porpoises are usually smaller and plumper than dolphins. Dolphins have a slender, beaklike snout. Porpoises have a much shorter snout.

There are about 35 different **species**, or types, of dolphins. The best known is probably the bottlenose dolphin, which is often seen in marine parks and aquariums. Other dolphin species include spinner, spotted, and striped dolphins. Although generally considered a whale, the largest member of the dolphin family is the orca, or killer whale. Dolphins live in groups called schools or **pods**. The pod of dolphins hunts together. These **predators** spread out to surround a **shoal** of fish and herd them tightly together. Then they take turns plunging into the center for a meal.

There are six species of porpoises. In the wild, porpoises usually live and hunt alone. Species include the harbor porpoise and vaquita.

A small pod of spotted dolphins searches for fish in the warm waters around the Bahamas.

River dolphins, such as this Amazon dolphin, are very rare.

Suited to Water

Dolphins and porpoises are found in most seas and oceans with the exception of icy polar waters. They mostly live around coasts, rather than out in the open sea. From the tip of its beak to its strong flippers and powerful tail, a dolphin is shaped to cut through the water. Even its eyes are suited to life in water. The animal produces a special fluid that keeps the outside of the eyes clean and moist.

Most dolphins and porpoises have a dark back and a pale belly. From above, the dark back is hard to see against the dark ocean surface. From below, the light belly is almost invisible against the bright, shimmering surface. This natural disguise, or **countershading**, helps dolphins approach their prey without being seen. It also makes it difficult for the dolphins to be seen by predators. Some dolphins also have beautiful swirly lines of color on the sides of their body. These markings also help break up the outline of the dolphins and **camouflage** them.

Brain Boxes

Dolphins are smart. They can perform all sorts of complicated tricks. They also respond to people in a lively way. In fact, dolphins seem to be just as interested in humans as humans are interested in them.

But exactly how smart are dolphins? It's hard for scientists to judge, because the dolphin's watery world is so different from ours. Tests show that young dolphins can learn to solve problems. For example, the dolphins had to remember which combinations of colors and simples shapes, such as circles and squares, would result in a reward of a tasty fish snack. The dolphins were better than most children at remembering the combinations! The dolphins that do the best on the tests are usually young ones that have been raised in **captivity**.

A dolphin trainer dives into an aquarium. Many people find swimming with dolphins to be an amazing experience.

21

A baby bottlenose dolphin stays close to its mother.

Dolphin Talk

Dolphins mainly communicate through sound. They can produce a wide range of noises, including squawks, squeaks, clicks, groans, and whistles. All these noises mean different things, so dolphins can use sounds to send very complicated messages. They can warn others of danger, call for help, or announce that they are ready to **mate**.

Young dolphins begin to "talk" soon after their birth. As they grow up, each develops its own particular whistle, called a signature whistle. Dolphins use these whistles to identify one another—similar to someone calling out his or her name in the dark. They whistle to one another when they are hunting. Each dolphin announces its position as the group spreads out to surround a shoal of fish. That helps coordinate the hunt. Scientists are beginning to understand dolphin talk, and one day they hope to be able to talk back to the dolphins!

Training Dolphins

In aquariums and marine shows, dolphins can be trained to do almost anything! They can leap through a hoop, touch a target, splash along upright on their tail, and perform many other tricks. Training a dolphin involves two main steps—signaling and reinforcing.

Trainers give a signal to tell the dolphin it is time to perform a certain action. The signal may be a whistle, a touch of the hand, or a spoken command, such as "GO!" Reinforcing involves rewarding the dolphin when it does the action, requested by the trainer. The dolphin learns that if it responds in a particular way to the signal, it gets a treat, such as a fish. Through repeating these three steps of signal, action, and reinforcement, over and over again, dolphins can learn a whole series of moves that will impress audiences at a show.

Dolphins at Risk

Dolphins and porpoises face many dangers in the wild. Some fall prey to larger hunters such as orcas, but the biggest danger comes from humans. Every year, thousands of dolphins die after being trapped in nets intended to catch fish such as tuna.

When a fishing fleet at sea discovers a nearby school of tuna, the fishers lower their nets. Dolphins often swim with tuna, and often get trapped, too. Once ensnared in the net, the dolphins cannot reach the water's surface to breathe. They quickly drown. Nowadays, some fishing boats use special nets that dolphins can see and avoid. Some nets even have hatches, through which trapped dolphins can escape. Cans containing tuna that have been caught in this way are labelled "dolphin friendly."

The distinctive white beluga is sometimes called the sea canary because of its high-pitched squeaks. This whale grows up to 15 feet (5 m) long.

The Whale Family

Whales are among the most amazing creatures on Earth. Some dive to the dark ocean depths, at more than 3,500 feet (1.1 km) down. Many spend their life traveling long distances in the open ocean.

Whales vary in size—from small belugas to giant sperm and blue whales. There are more than 80 different species of whales. Scientists divide them into two main groups: toothed whales and **baleen** whales. Toothed whales include sperm and beaked whales, dolphins, and porpoises. All these whales feed on fish and other prey, which they track using echolocation.

Baleen whales have no teeth. Instead, huge, horny plates, called baleen, hang down inside their mouth. The whales use the baleen like a giant **sieve**, straining small fish, krill, and shrimp from the seawater. Baleen whales include gray, blue, and humpback whales.

A humpback mother pushes her newly born baby up to the water's surface so it can breathe air.

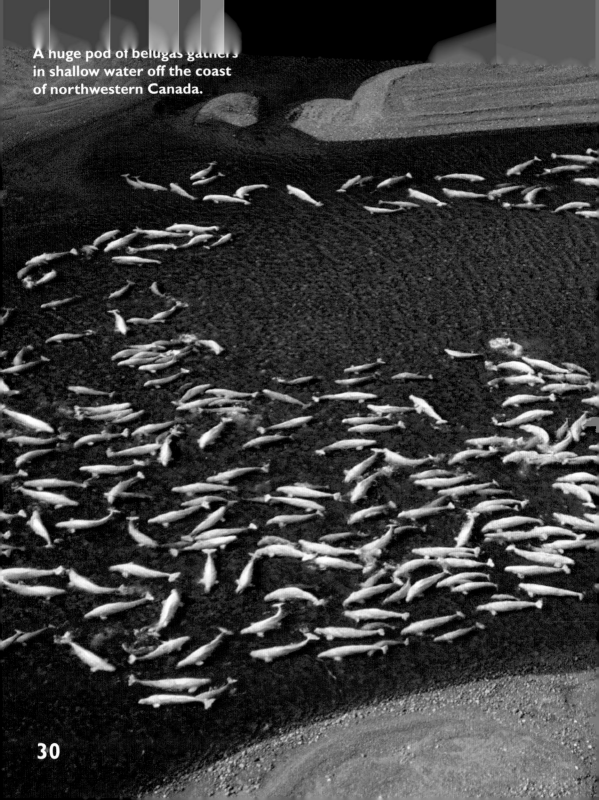

A huge pod of belugas gathers in shallow water off the coast of northwestern Canada.

Living in Groups

Some whales are loners, but most live in pods, or schools. Like dolphins, other kinds of whales in a pod use sound to communicate to one another, too. They let out sighs, groans, clicks, squeals, and roars to express their intentions and feelings.

Whales are affectionate and loyal. Some types have been seen swimming along together with flippers touching, as if holding hands. The whales in a pod will work together to help any group member that is injured or in trouble. Whales and dolphins can also be playful. They like to swim along in the waves made by ships and other watercraft. They also seem to enjoy the low hum of a ship's engine!

Whale Intelligence

Like dolphins, whales are clever creatures. The brain of the great whales is huge! A sperm whale's brain weighs about 20 pounds (9 kg). In comparison, an average human brain weighs just 3 pounds (1.4 kg). However, it is not the size of the brain alone that indicates intelligence, but the size of the brain compared to the size of the body. Humans have a bigger brain than whales compared to overall body size.

Captive whales can be taught to perform tasks and tricks. Whales also show their intelligence in the complicated "language" they use to communicate with one another. Research has shown that each pod of killer whales has its own particular way of speaking. This is similar to the accents of people living in a particular part of a country, who have their own phrases not used elsewhere.

A pod of orcas swims close to the Alaskan coast. In the wild, orcas can live to more than 60 years.

An orca snaps up a sea lion on a beach in Argentina.

Beautiful Killers

The orca, also called the killer whale, has beautiful markings, with handsome white patches on its smooth, jet-black skin. Orcas are toothed whales and part of the dolphin family. Like other dolphins, orcas live in pods.

True to its name, the orca is indeed a killer. It goes after all sorts of prey, ranging from fish, squid, and birds to seals and dolphins. Orcas will even sometimes wriggle a short way up the beach to snatch a seal. They sometimes toy with a captured seal like a cat playing with a mouse, tossing it high in the air before eating it. Surprisingly, orcas can also be gentle. Captive orcas can be trained and trusted with humans in their pool. They are a popular attraction in many aquariums.

Blue Whales

The gigantic blue whale—bigger than any known dinosaur—takes its name from its bluish-gray **mottled** skin. Like many other sea mammals, blue whales have countershading, with a dark upper surface and a paler belly and underside of the flippers. Folds, or grooves, extend from under the whale's chin to its belly. Blue whales belong to a group of baleen whales known as rorquals (RAW-KWULZ). Other members in this group include minke, fin, and humpback whales.

There are three kinds, or subspecies, of blue whales. Northern blue whales live in the North Pacific and North Atlantic oceans. Southern blue whales are found in the oceans of the southern hemisphere. Pygmy blue whales—which are still a whopping 80 feet (24 m) long—live in the southern Indian Ocean and South Pacific.

Blue whales live alone, except for mothers with calves. They eat krill—up to several tons of these crustaceans each day. Blue whale calves weigh about 6,000 pounds (2,700 kg) at birth and drink 850 pints (400 l) of milk each day.

Blue whales can swim at speeds of up to 30 miles (50 km) per hour.

A humpback whale breaches off the coast of Alaska.

Humpback Whales

Humpback whales, like blue whales, are also rorquals. Their name comes from the appearance of their rounded back when they dive. Humpback whales have dark skin except on the grooves below their mouth and on their flippers, which are much paler. The edges of their tail fins are jagged, or scalloped. Their flippers are very long and can be almost a third of the body length. Unusually for a mammal, female humpback whales are larger than the males. They can grow to 50 feet (16 m) long and weigh about 64 tons (65 tonnes).

Humpbacks live in pods. They travel between the tropics and Arctic feeding grounds each year. In the breeding season, the male humpback whale broadcasts his need for a mate by singing. He hangs in the water for hours, producing long streams of sighs, squeals, and moans. Humpbacks are often seen leaping out of the water, or breaching. Scientists think they do that to warn the other members of the pod of danger or to attract mates.

Protecting Whales

Whales have been hunted by humans for thousands of years. For generations, Arctic peoples, such as the Inuit, have hunted whales for their meat. They also use the whales' fatty blubber, which can be burned in oil lamps. However, Arctic people never killed very many whales.

From the 1700s on, whaling became big business. Soon many nations around the world were hunting whales. At first, the whalers used handheld weapons called harpoons to kill the whales. But at about the beginning of the 1900s, the harpoon-gun was invented. This powerful weapon made it much easier for whalers to pierce the skin and blubber of whales to kill them.

By the mid-1900s, so many whales had been killed that many species were in danger of dying out. The whaling nations formed an organization to try to solve this problem. The organization recommended a ban on whaling. Now almost all countries have given up whaling, and whale numbers have started to rise again.

Some countries still practice whaling. These include Japan, Norway, Iceland, Canada, and the United States (in Alaska).

41

Elephant seals get their name not only from their great size but also from the male's long nose.

The Seal Family

Many people find seals very cute and appealing. This is probably because seals have a doglike face. There are 35 species of seals. They vary greatly in size—the smallest is the 5-foot (1.5-m) Arctic ringed seal, which weighs 100 pounds (45 kg). The largest is the elephant seal, which grows up to 21 feet (6.5 m) long and weighs up to 4 tons (4 tonnes). Seals eat a variety of animals, such as fish, squid, shellfish, and birds.

Scientists divide the seal family into three main groups. These are true—or earless—seals, eared seals, and the walrus. In fact, all seals have ears, but "earless" seals have no visible ear flaps, only an opening leading to the inner ear. The earless group includes elephant seals and leopard seals. Eared seals include sea lions and fur seals.

Walruses are so different from other seals that scientists put them in a group of their own. They grow up to 10½ feet (3.2 m) long and can weigh 3,500 pounds (1,600 kg). Walruses have tusks and whiskers, which they use to root about on the seabed in search of shellfish.

Seals on Duty

Seals and sea lions are clever, like dolphins. They are also skilled divers, fast swimmers, and nimble on land. In the wild, they spend a lot of their time on rocky coasts. In sea shows and aquariums, seals and sea lions can be trained to do all sorts of tricks and acrobatics. In zoos, people love to watch seals and sea lions at feeding time. The agile animals easily catch fish tossed to them by their keepers.

Some seals have done active duty in the U.S. Navy! In 1968, the Navy's Undersea Center in Hawaii began to use sea lions in a project called Quick Find. The project trained sea lions to recover equipment that had been lost at sea. They proved perfect for this kind of work because they can dive deep and stay underwater for a long time.

A sea lion can dive to depths of 900 feet (275 m) when hunting.

This sea cow is known as
a West Indian manatee.

Sea Cows

The family of sea cows is made up of three species of manatees and the dugong. Sea cows look a lot like large seals. However, they are not closely related to seals. In fact, their closest living relatives are elephants.

Sea cows have a large, plump body and a smallish head with a whiskered snout. They are the only sea mammals that are vegetarian. They use their tail and long flippers to swim slowly through warm, coastal waters, munching water plants. They need to graze on a lot of underwater plants to survive—up to 15 percent of their own body weight each day. That could be as much as 500 pounds (230 kg) of vegetation a day for West Indian manatees. These are the largest type of sea cow, growing to 15 feet (4.5 m) long and weighing up to 3,500 pounds (1,600 kg).

A fifth species of sea cow, called Steller's sea cow, was hunted to **extinction** by humans in the 1700s. It lived in the northern Pacific Ocean and grazed on seaweed. This giant sea cow grew to almost 26 feet (8 m) long.

In the Future

Humans have not always behaved well toward sea mammals. Over the centuries, people have hunted them for their meat, blubber and, in the case of seals, their fur. Carelessly, humans have allowed some species to almost die out altogether. In many countries, wildlife organizations are now working to give seals, whales, and other sea mammals a better future in the wild.

In aquariums and marine parks, sea mammals delight visitors with their skill and intelligence. There's no doubt that these mammals can be trained to a high level. Many people have become involved in helping sea mammals after admiring them in captivity. However, scientific studies suggest that these clever animals suffer if kept in too small a tank or aquarium. They also suffer if they are separated from their own kind. While progress is being made, much more work still needs to be done to ensure that sea mammals are well treated both in captivity and in the wild.

Words to Know

Baleen Horny plates that hang from the upper jaw of some whales. They are used to strain food from the water.

Blowholes The openings on the top of a whale's head that act as nostrils.

Blubber A layer of thick fat under the skin.

Camouflage Colorations or patterns on an animal that allows it to blend into its surroundings.

Captivity When an animal is kept in a zoo, a nature park, or someone's home and is not free to roam in the wild.

Counter-shading The color patterning of many water animals, in which the underside is pale and the back is dark.

Echolocation A technique for finding food underwater. The animal sends out sounds and listens for echoes that bounce back off its prey.

Extinction When all of a kind of animal has died and gone forever.

Flippers The front limbs of a sea mammal.

49

Gills	The feathery structures in a fish's head that allow it to absorb oxygen from water.
Hibernate	To spend winter in a deep sleep.
Mammals	Animals that have hair on their body and feed their young on milk.
Mate	To come together to produce young.
Migrations	Long, regular journeys made by animals to escape cold or find food or a safe place to breed.
Mottled	Patchy or spotted coloration.
Pods	Groups of whales or dolphins.
Predators	Animals that hunt other animals.
Prey	An animal that is eaten by another.
Shoal	A group of fish.
Sieve	A utensil with a mesh that separates larger particles from smaller ones.
Species	The scientific word for animals of the same type that breed together.

Find Out More

Books

Rhodes, M. J., and D. Hall. *Dolphins, Seals, And Other Sea Mammals*. Undersea Encounters. Danbury, Connecticut: Children's Press, 2007.

Thomas, P. *Marine Mammal Preservation*. Science of Saving. Brookfield, Connecticut: Millbrook Press, 2000.

Web sites

The Marine Mammal Center—Kids Only!
www.marinemammalcenter.org/juniormembership/index.html
A lot of information about protecting wild sea mammals.

Marine Mammal Printouts
www.enchantedlearning.com/subjects/mammals/marinemammals/Marinemammalprintouts.shtml
More than 25 printouts of marine mammals to color in.

Index